Beautiful or

You have a heart full of love for others. It will not go unnoticed.

Hebrews 6:10:

For God, the Faithful One, is not unfair. How can he forget the beautiful work you have done for him? He remembers the love you demonstrate as you continually serve his beloved ones for the glory of his name.

I love you.
Mom

2022

AS IT IS
IN HEAVEN

REVELATION 4 + 5

Bob Perry & Amy Joy Lykosh

MAKARIOS
PRESS

Esmont, VA

Makarios Press
P.O. Box 28, Esmont, VA 22937

Scripture in NIV unless otherwise stated.

Cover & Book Design: Nate Braxton
Cover Illustration: Jonelle Lilly

ISBN 978-1-956561-00-5

Printed in the United States of America

CONTENTS

ABOUT THIS BOOK

Bob Perry has been praying out of Revelation 4 and 5 for decades.

In the scripture, Jesus taught his disciples to pray, "Your kingdom come, your will be done, on earth as it is in heaven."

But how can we know what we're praying for if we don't know about heaven?

That's the beauty of Revelation 4 and 5. John the Apostle gives us a vision of what's happening in heaven: a world of worship and praise to the Lord, a picture of the incredible worthiness of the Lamb who was slain.

This beautiful picture almost defies description.

Here we'll unpack the heavenly scene, using free verse poetry.

After some introductory material, and a quick overview of Revelation 1-3, this book goes through the entire text of Revelation 4 and 5, verse-by-verse, and sometimes word-by-word.

Each poem includes, in italics, the specific words of scripture that the rest of the poem explores.

We pray that you come away enthralled anew with the beauty of the Lord.

INTRODUCTION
Why Revelation?

The Problem

At the first,
Such love and friendship,
Such rapid, amazing growth.

"Lord, I want to be your friend.
I want to worship and praise from a pure heart.
I don't want to be distracted.
I don't want to sing when my heart is far away."

Then comes the subtle shift.

In the midst of worship,
The mind wanders,
Focused on

Just about anything

But

The magnificent Lord.

Working Hard

Instead of *being with* Jesus, like Mary,
We start *doing for* Jesus, like Martha.

Less romance,
More duty.

Christ himself, no longer the priority and passion.
Instead, the work we do for him.

As we work harder,
The heart slips farther.

The works we imagine he prizes
Become lifeless burdens to us

Until,
In the end,
We become

Bone dry,
Hard,
Bored ...

Cynical.

Is there no balm in Gilead?

First Calling

Question 1: What is the chief end of man?
Answer: Man's chief end is to glorify God, and to
enjoy him forever.[1]

The calling of worship
Surpasses that of
Apostle,
Prophet,
Evangelist,
Pastor,
Teacher.

Let a convert first become a
Worshipper,
And only then become a
Worker.

Workers who don't know how to worship are
Marked by the smell of sweat from fleshly toil.

Worship first.
Then work bears
The fragrance of grace
And the sound of eternity.

Worship brings a flow of life.
It carries our best to the heart of God,
And delivers his life and blessing back.

A true worshiper never remains in a dead state.

Make a wrong decision?
Sometimes.

Fall down?
On occasion.

But a worshipper comes back,
Because of the desperate need for the
kindness of God.

Work, Transformed

God rewards
Even a small step toward him.

As he becomes
The focus of life,

Work becomes the life-giving overflow
Of passion for Christ

Instead of just
Draining busyness in an attempt to please him.

Chapter One
GET ORIENTED

Part of the Lord's Prayer

Jesus prayed,
Your kingdom come,
Your will be done,
On earth as it is in heaven.[2]

How do we pray
For God's kingdom to come
If we don't know what it looks like?

Solution:
Scenes from Revelation.

Consider well
And see more clearly
What to pray for.

Apocalyptic

Revelation.

Also known as
Apocalypse.

Unveil,
Unfold,
Uncover,
Reveal,

Things not previously known.

Things which cannot be known
Apart from the unveiling.

Author

John, last survivor of the original twelve disciples.

Judas killed himself.
The others all martyred.

Jesus' most intimate friend on earth,
The disciple Jesus loved.

Exiled to the island of Patmos,
There he wrote of his Savior.

Not as a flat, one-dimensional character.
Not an ancient icon.

Rather, a complex person
With more facets and more sparkle
Than the finest-cut diamond.

Gospel, Revelation

John wrote two narratives:
His eponymous gospel, and Revelation.

When John wrote
His gospel of Jesus,

He called Jesus the *logos*, the Word.
The Lamb of God.

The Lamb who was slain
To take away the sins of the world.

When John wrote
Revelation,

He called Jesus
The Lamb of God.

Seated on a throne,
High and exalted.

In the book of John:
Jesus as the Son of Man.

In the book of Revelation:
Jesus as the Eternal One, the Son of God.

Not About the Bad Guy

What comes to mind
When you think about Revelation?

The dragon?
The lake of fire?

Though these both show up briefly,
Reframe your expectation.

Revelation reveals
Christ in his majestic, glorified power.

By one count, twenty-seven songs
In twenty-two chapters,

Focusing on the splendor
Of the eternal King.

Disclosure?

Considering Revelation
Is supposed to be

The revelation,
The disclosure,
The report,
The announcement

From Jesus Christ ...

It is surprisingly challenging to understand.

Yes, Jesus said
He spoke in parables

That they may be ever seeing
But never perceiving,

And ever hearing
But never understanding.[3]

So the scripture has
Precedent for
Purposeful
Confusion.

But still!

Is there a better way to
Perceive and
Understand?

It is the glory of God to conceal a matter;
To search out a matter is the glory of kings.[4]

Come and
Search.

Contrast

John shows us
Jesus Christ as victorious Lord of all.

See the striking
Contrast

Between earth and
Heaven,

Between time and
Eternity,

Between evil and
Good,

Between illusion and
Reality,

Between lies and
Truth,

Between the kingdom of darkness and the
Kingdom of light.

The temporal world on earth,
Contrasted with the eternity of heaven.

Exhortation

Revelation is a book of truth,
A book of insight.

Read with a growing confidence
That this is a book about

The God who is in charge.

See that
Christ will come again,
To establish his kingdom of
Righteousness and
Perfect justice.

The kingdom of the world has become
The kingdom of our Lord and of his Messiah,
And he will reign for ever and ever.[5]

He will triumph over evil.

This coming King,
This Savior,
This Lord and Christ,
This Anointed One,
This Lord of all,

Is trustworthy.

Is worthy.

More Than Prophecy

In Revelation
Find a telling of future events,
Prophetic foretelling.

But more than that, find
Proclamation.

Read to find out

Who God is,
His character,

And

What he will do,
His action.

Why It Matters

Revelation is a book about the future,
Yes.

But it is also a book about the present.

Jesus Christ is the same
Yesterday and
Today and
Forever.[6]

Offered now:
Hope to all believers.

All suffering,
Pain,
Rejection,
Even death ...

Swallowed up in victory.

The triumph of
Christ's death and

Resurrection.

Center / Centered

We live in the shakiness of earth,
Even as we pray
"Your kingdom come,
Your will be done."
Bring the stability of heaven here.

Revelation shows that
Christ is the coming conqueror.
He is the King of kings,
The Lord of lords,
And he will defeat all evil.

The one we worship
Is the center of all.
He sits on the throne
And rules in power,
Ever in control.

As we gaze on what is to come,
In the midst of our
Shakiness,
We become

Centered.

Preparation

One day we will meet
The Savior
Face to face.

For now, we have the opportunity
To discover who he is.

The revelation in Revelation
Helps prepare us
For that day when we will be
Before the Lord himself;

The great and dreadful day
When we will be
Before the God of heaven,
The God of Earth.

Now is the day of preparation.

Eternity begins

Now.

Proper Focus

Solomon asked,
Famously,
For wisdom.

And yet, with all his wisdom,
His days did not end well.
And so was that request
As wise as it could have been?

Solomon's father David made a single request, too,
The generation before.

One thing I ask from the Lord,
This only do I seek:
That I may dwell in the house of the Lord
All the days of my life,
To gaze on the beauty of the Lord
And to seek him in his temple.[7]

David, the man after God's own heart.
Presumably, his request was the better choice.

Now ...

What a gift:

In Revelation, the chance
To see

What David longed to see:

The beauty of the Lord,
In his temple.

Great and Terrible

And now, prepare yourself.

Stop seeking precise meaning in signs
and symbols.
Put aside questions of day and time and season.

Enter in to the great and terrible scene
With a renewed sense of wonder.

Chapter Two
SETTING THE STAGE

Revelation: Beginning

The revelation from Jesus Christ, which God gave him to show his servants what must soon take place.[8]

No common book here.

This is the word of the Lord.
Thanks be to God.

Blessed

*Blessed is the one who reads aloud the words of this
prophecy, and blessed are those who hear it and
take to heart what is written in it, because the
time is near.*[9]

Blessed.

The Greek word *makarios*.[10]

Happiness.
Contentment.

Knowing your place in the world,
And satisfaction in that place.

Being in your happy place.

A fair translation:

You are in your happy place
When you read aloud the words of this prophecy.

In the Spirit

On the Lord's Day I was in the Spirit

Four times in Revelation
John writes, *I was in the Spirit.*[11]
The Holy Spirit opened his heart to another realm,
Gave him insight of what is and is to come.

Above all, you must understand that
No prophecy of Scripture came about
By the prophet's own
Interpretation of things.

For prophecy never had its origin
In the human will,
But prophets, though human, spoke from God
As they were carried along by the Holy Spirit.[12]

A Trumpet

I heard behind me a loud voice like a trumpet

A modern trumpet:
Brassy and bold,
Metallic and man-made.

In ancient Israel, a different instrument:
The shofar, a ram's horn,
Naturally grown, made of keratin.

Strong, melodic,
Full of passion,
Rich with love and affection.

Think About This Voice

like a trumpet

Commanding and loud.
Triumphant.

A trumpet sounds
Both

"Reveille" in the morning,
Energetic and exhilarating, and

"Taps" at night,
Comforting and soothing.

Compelling,
Clear,

Confident,
Courageous.

Sincere and
Strong,

This voice
Stirs the slothful heart.

Not a Voice Over

I turned around to see the voice that
  was speaking to me.

The voice behind
Did not boom out of nothingness.

Not incorporeal
Like thunder.

Not a disembodied
Voice over.

John turned to see
A visible being.

Pregnant with Meaning

And when I turned I saw seven golden lampstands,
    and among the lampstands was someone like a
    son of man

In the Old Testament,
Daniel spoke of this same person.

In my vision at night I looked,
And there before me was one
Like a son of man,

Coming with the clouds of heaven.
He approached the Ancient of Days
And was led into his presence.

He was given authority,
Glory and
Sovereign power;

All nations and peoples
Of every language
Worshiped him.

His dominion is
An everlasting dominion
That will not pass away,

And his kingdom is one
That will never be destroyed.[13]

Description

*And when I turned I saw seven golden lampstands,
and among the lampstands was someone like a
son of man*

His clothing: a foot-length robe, with a golden
sash around his chest.

His hair: white like wool, like snow.

His eyes: like blazing fire.

His feet: like bronze glowing in a furnace.

His voice: like the sound of rushing waters.

His right hand: held seven stars.

His mouth: from it came forth a sharp,
double-edged sword.

His face: like the sun shining in all its brilliance.

The Voice, Described Anew

and his voice was like the sound of rushing waters

Waters rush in spring,
When snow melts and
Rivers race.

The rushing waters
Thrust aside
All obstacles.

Movement.
Energy.
Life.

Abundance.
More.
Plenty ...

Coming.

Identity

When I saw him, I fell at his feet as though dead.

Then he placed his right hand on me and said:

"Do not be afraid.
I am the First and the Last.
I am the Living One;

I was dead, and now look,
I am alive for ever and ever!

And I hold the keys of death and Hades."

Jesus.

With John,
We fall at your feet.

Speak over us, too.

Instructions

Write, therefore, what you have seen, what is now and what will take place later. The mystery of the seven stars that you saw in my right hand and of the seven golden lampstands is this: The seven stars are the angels of the seven churches, and the seven lampstands are the seven churches.

Seven churches in Asia:
Strengths.
Weaknesses.
Compliments.
Censure.
Encouragement.
Caution.

Ephesus.
Smyrna.
Pergamon.
Thyatira.
Sardis.
Philadelphia.
Laodicea.

Write
To the angel
Of each church.
Whoever has ears,
Let them hear
What the Spirit says
To the churches.

Transition

From the churches that were,
To the Church that is and is to come,
Celebrate the transition
From chapter three to chapter four.

The rest of Revelation details
John's vision,
Similar in places to Daniel's vision,
Ezekiel's vision.

The Lord God
Will defeat all evil.
He will conquer.
He will win.

As followers of God live
In obedience to Jesus Christ,
The coming conqueror and judge,
His triumph becomes ours.

Chapter Three
REVELATION 4:1-7

An Open Door

*After this I looked, and there before me was a door
standing open in heaven.*

An open door,
An invitation.

A closed door says:
Stay away.

Or, at the very least:
Wait.

An open door says:
Come in.
Welcome.
I desire your presence.
I want you.
I like you.
I have more for you.

The invitation:
Enter in.

The Greatest Invitation

And the voice I had first heard speaking to me like a
*   trumpet said, "Come up here,"*

What an invitation!
Come up here.
John knew Jesus,

The son of man,
Born of a virgin,
Flesh and blood.

He was about to see Jesus,
The son of God,
Seated in the heavens.

Like Moses

"Come up here,"

Centuries before,
The Lord descended
To the top of Mount Sinai
And called Moses
To the top of the mountain.
So Moses went up.[14]

Aaron, too,
Was included in the invitation.
But the priests
And the people
Must not force their way through
To come up to the Lord,
Or he will break out against them.

Centuries later,
The Lord spoke to John
To come up.

And we get to witness with John!
No need to force our way through.
No threat of destruction against us.

Simply an invitation to
Witness,

Too.

Inexorable

and I will show you what must take place after this.

What must take place.

No question.
No "perhaps."

Rather,
Inexorable.
Required.

The absolute guaranteed result.

The scene was set in motion
When the Lamb was slain.

The scene was set in motion
And it will not be denied.

Join In

At once I was in the Spirit,

Though John saw these things
With his own eyes
In the Spirit,

He writes them for our benefit,
That we, too,
May be in the Spirit
With him.

Thanks be to God.

Enthroned

and there before me was a throne

The supremacy and certainty
Of God's plan and power.

With God on the throne,
No question who rules the earth.

God reigns over the nations;
God is seated on his holy throne.[15]

An Earthly Throne

in heaven

In St. Petersburg, Russia,
Peter the Great's Winter Palace
Boasts 1,000 rooms.

Want to see the throne room?

Enter by the grand entrance.
Walk up the grand staircase.

The throne room,
Larger than two basketball courts,
Its ceiling reflects
The intricate floor patterns,
Crafted from five different types of wood.

Behold the greatness of the Czar of Russia.

And yet ...

How much greater the heavenly throne,
The heavenly King!

Describing the Indescribable

and there before me was a throne in heaven

The prophet Micaiah:
I saw the Lord sitting on his throne
With all the multitudes of heaven
Standing around him
On his right and on his left.[16]

The prophet Ezekiel:
Above the vault over their heads was
What looked like a throne of lapis lazuli.[17]

The prophet Isaiah:
I saw the Lord seated on a throne,
High and exalted,
And the train of his robe filled the temple.
Above him were seraphs,
Each with six wings:
With two wings they covered their faces,
With two they covered their feet,
And with two they were flying.[18]

The train of his robe filled the temple!

This throne is not in a palace,
But a temple.

Worship this God.

Someone

with someone sitting on it.

John knew Jesus,
Perhaps better than any.

On earth, he sat with his head on Jesus' breast.
Called himself "the disciple Jesus loved."

And yet, in this place of splendor,
He writes, simply,

Someone

Sits on the throne.

Indescribable.
How much splendor and majesty

Jesus left behind to come, disguised,
To earth.

Jewel-Like Appearance

And the one who sat there had the appearance of
jasper and ruby.

Though jasper today is opaque,
Colored yellow, green, red, or brown,
Revelation 21:11 calls it "clear as crystal."

Have you seen a clear crystal sparkle
In the light
With the colors of the rainbow?
Joyful beauty.
Magnificent.

Ruby:
A blood red, translucent gem.

The one who sat there had the appearance,
Not of a Hebrew man,
But a difficult-to-describe,
Difficult-to-imagine,
Shimmering,
Intense,
Glory.

Emerald Halo

A rainbow that shone like an emerald encircled
the throne.

The rainbow: a sign of God's covenant with man.
The scattered light and color reminds us that
His mercy and love cover all.

Did the rainbow shine green?
Or was an emerald simply an ancient example of
glorious brightness?

About 700 years before John's vision,
The prophet Ezekiel, too, wrote of the
throne room.

A figure like that of a man.
I saw that from what appeared to be his waist up
He looked like glowing metal,
As if full of fire,
And that from there down he looked like fire;
And brilliant light surrounded him.

Like the appearance of a rainbow in the clouds
On a rainy day,
So was the radiance around him.

This was the appearance
Of the likeness
Of the glory of the LORD.[19]

Get a glimpse of God's true nature.
Be enthralled forever.

King of Kings

*Surrounding the throne were twenty-four other thrones,
and seated on them were twenty-four elders.*

What does it mean to be King of kings
And Lord of lords?

Having twenty-four
Crowned kings surround your throne

Seems like
At least the beginning of a definition.

Speculation

and seated on them were twenty-four elders.

Who were these twenty-four elders?

Perhaps a representative
Of each of the twelve tribes of Israel
And the twelve apostles.

Dovetail
Together

The Old Testament
And the New,
The Old Covenant
And the New.

Most likely they represent
All of the redeemed of God for all time,
Both before and after
Christ's death and resurrection.

Jews and Gentiles all redeemed,
Now all part of God's family,
All bowing in worship.

All that passed on earth,
All success, prestige, position,
Ceases to matter before the throne.

Now
Bow.

Clothing

They were dressed in white

In the West,
A bride wears white,

Symbolizing
Purity.
Holiness.
Hope.

The elders, too, wear white.

The bride of Christ,
Clothed in righteousness.

Redeemed.
Renewed.

Glorified and
Glorifying God.

Clothed

*They were dressed in white and had crowns of gold on
their heads.*

White robes:
No longer sin-stained,
But undefiled priestly garments of worship.

Gold crowns:
The King remembers and rewards
Service and deeds done from a pure heart.

Emanating

*From the throne came flashes of lightning, rumblings
and peals of thunder.*

See it.
Hear it.

Lightning flash.
Thunder crash.

Beauty and glory in
Lights, colors, shadows.

More enthralling than
The most fabulous fireworks display.

Divine power
Demonstrated.

The fear of the Lord.
Not in terror, but in

Submission.
Awe.

Worship.
Reverence.

Lightning and Thunder

From the throne came flashes of lightning, rumblings
and peals of thunder.

When the ancient Israelites
Came to Mount Sinai,
The Lord came close
With thunder and lightning
And a thick cloud.[20]

Then God gave his people
His laws.

Lightning and thunder
At a significant event.

Your thunder was heard in the whirlwind,
Your lightning lit up the world;
The earth trembled and quaked.[21]

God's power and majesty
Burst forth.

A significant event
At all times.

Lamps

In front of the throne, seven lamps were blazing.

A lamp brings

Light.
Heat.
Fire.
Guidance.

A partial description of
The work of
The Holy Spirit.

Zechariah Saw This, Too

In front of the throne, seven lamps were blazing.

When an angel awoke
The prophet Zechariah,
The angel asked the man,
"What do you see?"

*"I see a solid gold lampstand
With a bowl at the top
And seven lamps on it,
With seven channels to the lamps....
What are these, my lord?"*

*"This is the word of the Lord
To Zerubbabel,
He who seeks to rebuild the Temple:
'Not by might,
Nor by power,
But by my Spirit,'
Says the Lord Almighty."*[22]

Not exactly a tidy mathematical equation,
This equals that.

An oblique answer.

Seven Spirits of God

These are the seven spirits of God.

Scripture speaks of the Holy Spirit.
But the seven spirits of God?

Four times Revelation
Mentions the seven spirits of God,
But offers no precise definition.

Perhaps Isaiah 11:2 gives the answer.

The Spirit of Yahweh will rest upon him,
The Spirit of Extraordinary Wisdom,
The Spirit of Perfect Understanding,
The Spirit of Wise Strategy,
The Spirit of Mighty Power,
The Spirit of Revelation, and
The Spirit of the Fear of Yahweh.[23]

When Glass Was Still Astonishing

*Also in front of the throne there was what looked like a
    sea of glass, clear as crystal.*

Today we buy glassware
And when it breaks we clean up the shards
And buy a replacement
And think no more of it.

And yet ...
To make glass, the worker must heat the kiln to
Eleven hundred degrees Fahrenheit,
A need for much wood and wind,
Not to mention sand and other minerals.

The Romans made glass,
But to get it crystal-clear?
Nearly impossible.

The sea of glass,
Highlights and reflects God's

Magnificence.
Holiness.
Majesty.
Beauty.
Might.
Splendor.
Greatness.
Significance.
Elegance.

Imagine the scene of throne and all
Mirrored on the sea.

Like a mountain scene in fall,
Duplicated in the clear waters of the central lake.

Picture this scene with
Awe.

Stand
Astonished.

Four Living Creatures

In the center, around the throne, were four living
*   creatures, and they were covered with eyes, in front*
*   and in back.*

The four creatures,
Guarding God's throne.

Ezekiel described these creatures, in
greater detail.[24]
In appearance their form was human,
But each of them had four faces and four wings.
Their legs were straight;
Their feet were like those of a calf
And gleamed like burnished bronze.
Under their wings on their four sides
They had human hands.
All four of them had faces and wings,
And the wings of one touched the wings of another.
Each one went straight ahead;
They did not turn as they moved.

The appearance of the living creatures
Was like burning coals of fire
Or like torches.
Fire moved back and forth among the creatures;
It was bright,
And lightning flashed out of it.
The creatures sped back and forth
Like flashes of lightning....
Full of eyes all around.

Chapter Four
REVELATION 4:8

Four Mighty

*The first living creature was like a lion, the second was
like an ox, the third had a face like a man, the fourth
was like a flying eagle.*

The mightiest among wild animals?
The lion.
Think: majesty and power and dominion.

The mightiest among domestic animals?
The ox.
Think: strength and faithfulness and loyalty.

The mightiest of all?
Man.
Think: creativity and intelligence and emotions.

The mightiest among birds?
The eagle.
Think: sovereignty and freedom and vision.

Wings and Eyes

Each of the four living creatures had six wings and was
covered with eyes all around, even under its wings.

Isaiah the prophet saw the same beings.
Above him were seraphim,
Each with six wings:
With two wings they covered their faces,
With two they covered their feet,
And with two they were flying.[25]

Their entire bodies,
Including their backs,
Their hands,
And their wings,
Were completely full of eyes.[26]

Imagine how much they could see with those eyes
All Around.

Unending

Day and night they never stop saying:

Day and night,
Night and day.

All the time.
Yes.

But look again:

They

Never

Stop.

The scripture doesn't say that they never sleep.
That would be surprising enough.

But not only do they not sleep, but
They never stop.

They take no intermissions.
No short breaks.
No cessation of worship.
They require no rest or recreation.

Jesus said,
"Take my yoke upon you,
And learn of me;
For I am meek
And lowly in heart:
And ye shall find rest
Unto your souls."[27]

To weary man,
Jesus offered an intermission,

A cessation of labor,
Some rest and recreation.

But in heaven,
The worship is so life-giving
That the worship leaders
Require no break.

The Whole Saying

"'Holy, holy, holy
is the Lord God Almighty,'
who was, and is, and is to come."

Unending.

Holy

Holy, holy, holy

From a Greek word meaning
"An awful thing."

Sacred.
Set apart.
Pure.
Clean.
Blameless.
Sinless.
Upright.
Awe-full.
Reverence.
Veneration.
Worthy.
Incomparable majesty.
Hallowed.

Repetition

Holy, holy, holy

Repeated for

Emphasis, emphasis, emphasis.

Superlative

Holy, holy, holy

More than pure.
Transcendent beauty.

More than set apart.
Separate from everything called common.

More than beautiful.
Unparalleled in beauty.

Unbelievable.
Like no other.

Infinitely superior.

Lord

is the Lord

From a Greek word meaning
"Supremacy."

Master.
Owner.
Supreme in authority.
Controller.
Possessor.
Disposer.
Sovereign.
Prince.
Chief.
Emperor.

God

God

From a Greek word meaning
"The supreme divinity."

Deity.
The only and true God.

The Godhead:
God the Father.
God the Son.
God the Holy Spirit.

Almighty

Almighty

From two Greek words.

First:
All.

Second:
Power.
Dominion.
Strength.
Might.

All power.
All dominion.
All strength.
All might.

The All-Ruler.
All powerful.
Omnipotent.

He who holds sway over all things.

Variation: The Old Testament Song

"Holy, holy, holy
is the Lord God Almighty,'
who was, and is, and is to come."

The prophet Isaiah recorded
The song of heaven like this:

Holy, holy, holy is the LORD Almighty;
The whole earth is full of his glory.[28]

Holy: yes.

The LORD: yes.
The proper name
Of the one true God,
Jehovah, "the existing One."

Almighty: though in English,
This appears to be the same word,
It offers a different shade of meaning
In the Hebrew than the Greek.

The LORD of hosts.

The LORD of an army,
Whether human or angelic.
The LORD of creation.
The LORD of war and warfare.

The entire earth
Is entirely full
Of his

Glory.

Entirely full
Of his

Abundance.
Copiousness.
Riches.
Weight.
Splendor.
Honor.
Dignity.
Reputation.
Reverence.

Past, Present, Future

who was, and is, and is to come.

The book of Hebrews says that

Jesus Christ is the same

Yesterday and
Today and
Forever.[29]

The writer of Hebrews
Joined
The song of heaven.

Chapter Five
REVELATION 4:9–11

The Scene

Whenever the living creatures give
Glory,
Honor and
Thanks

To him who sits on the throne
And who lives for ever and ever,

The twenty-four elders
Fall

Down

Before him who sits on the throne
And worship him who lives for ever and ever.

They lay their crowns before the throne and say:

"You are worthy, our Lord and God,
To receive glory and honor and power,
For you created all things,
And by your will they were created
And have their being."

Same Scene,
Different Translation

Eugene Peterson, in *The Message*,
Tells it like this:

Every time the Animals gave
Glory and
Honor and
Thanks to

The One Seated on the Throne—
The age-after-age Living One—

The Twenty-four Elders would
Fall

Prostrate

Before the One Seated on the Throne.
They worshiped
The age-after-age Living One.

They threw their crowns at the foot of the
Throne, chanting,

Worthy, O Master! Yes, our God!
Take the glory!
The honor!
The power!
You created it all;

It was created because you wanted it.

Glory

Whenever the living creatures give glory,

The modern dictionary defines
Glory:

1. high renown or honor won by notable
   achievements.
2. magnificence or great beauty.

Not entirely satisfactory.

The Bible translates the Greek word:

Glory.
Glorious.
Honor.
Praise.
Dignity.
Worship.

Better.

Glory Again

Whenever the living creatures give glory,

A deeper dive into
Glory:

A good opinion, with the result of praise
and honor.

Splendor.
Brightness.
Magnificence.
Excellence.
Preeminence.
Dignity.
Grace.

Majesty.

Glory Again and Again

Whenever the living creatures give glory,

One definition of glory:
Majesty.

A deeper dive into
Majesty:

That which belongs to God as supreme ruler,
The absolute perfection of the deity.

That which belongs to Christ,
The kingly majesty of the Messiah,
The absolutely perfect personal excellency
    of Christ.

A most glorious condition.
A most exalted state.

Or, as one Bible dictionary said:

"Of that condition with God the Father in heaven
To which Christ was raised
After he had achieved his work on earth."[30]

Honor

honor,

Definitions, usage, translations:

Precious.
Price.
Money paid.
Sum.
A value.
Valuables.
A prized thing.
Preciousness.
Dignity.
Deference.
Reverence.
Veneration.
Esteem, especially of the highest degree.

Honor Again

honor,

Honor usually seems so
Ephemeral and intangible,

Like a courtly bow
Or the tip of a hat.

And yet this word also has shades of
Permanence and tangibility.

Valuables.
Worth.
Price.
Sum.

A tangible honor of payment.
The custom due.

Lord, you get all of the honor,
Both ephemeral and permanent,
Tangible and intangible.

The elders, prostrate,
Cast their crowns before you,

Giving you honor,
Both bowing and treasure.

Thanks

and thanks

From two Greek words meaning
"Good" and "rejoice" or "cheerful."

Thanksgiving.
Giving of thanks.
Thankfulness.
Gratitude.

The Lord's Supper,
Sometimes called
"Eucharist,"

From the Greek meaning
"Thanksgiving."

Same word.

Eucharist

thanks

Jesus offered
The bread and the wine,
His body,
To his followers.

He gives
The Eucharist.

We give thanks back to him.

We give him
The Eucharist.

Thank you, Jesus.

For Ever and Ever

*to him who sits on the throne and who lives for
    ever and ever,*

The High King,
For all time.

Even worldly kings recognize

His
Preeminence,

His
Permanence.

The prophet Daniel tells
Of Nebuchadnezzar,
An impressive king in his day,
But who praised the greater King.

*I praised the Most High;
I honored and glorified him who lives forever.
His dominion is
An eternal dominion;
His kingdom endures
From generation
To generation.*[31]

*He is the living God
And he endures forever;
His kingdom will not be destroyed,
His dominion
Will*

Never

End.[32]

Fall Down

the twenty-four elders fall down before him who sits on
the throne

The elders

Before God

Kneel.
Bow.
Lay prostrate.

Fall Down

the twenty-four elders fall down

How embarrassing to fall down.
A sign of weakness,
Clumsiness,
Accident,
Loss of control.

In the elderly,
A fall may even prove
Fatal.

Moreover,
Humans are
The only living beings
To walk upright
As their main mode of
Movement,
One of the unique aspects of man
Among creation.

When man falls down,
Lies down,
Are we not like
Any other animal?

Except.

How honoring,
To acknowledge another as stronger and better.

How humble,
To worship in reverent and terrible awe.

How human,
To be overcome with astonishment.

How proper,
To fall prostrate before the Great King.

Here a fall is not a negation of humanity,
But a sacrifice of praise.

An offering of all of ourselves,
Given to worship the Lord.

Lord, none can stand in your presence.
We are willing to be undone before you,
By how magnificent you are.

Effective Worship

*the twenty-four elders fall down before him who
  sits on the throne and worship him who lives for
  ever and ever.*

Enter into the very presence of God.
There grow
Relationship.
Intimacy.
Affection.
Knowledge.

Worship should affect
Our thoughts,
Our emotions.

The elders fall,
Not worried about their prestige,
Their position,
Their past.

Rather,
Fully consumed
With the desire to
Bring him
All the glory
That is due him.

Worship

and worship him who lives for ever and ever.

Not "worship" as exuberant singing.
Not "worship" as a religious observance.

No.

Here worship means:
"To kiss,
Like a dog licking his master's hand."

Think of how
Subservient.
Undignified.
Abandoned.

Adoring.

The word has overtones of
Fawning.
Crouching.
Prostration in homage.
Reverence.
Obeisance.
Adoration.

Think of a culture where
Commoners fall to their knees and
Touch their foreheads to the ground in
Profound reverence
To one of superior rank.

Casting Crowns

They lay their crowns before the throne

This is not a careful motion,
This laying down of crowns.

"Casting crowns" is a reasonable translation.

The same word in the scripture describes
Casting dead wood into a fire.
Peter casting nets into the sea.
Spoiled salt being cast out.

Think: to throw something
Without much concern for where it falls,
Without care for the result.

Throw down the crown
In absolute abandon.

The Crowns

their crowns

In ancient times,
The victor in a public game
Won a garland,
A circlet,
A prize,
Twined or wreathed around.

A crown.

An ornament to honor and celebrate.

All that they worked for,
All that they won,

The elders throw down
Before the throne.

Movement
In the song.

An Encounter

and say,

Not a boring declaration,
Mind elsewhere,
Bored and distracted.

No.

This focused speech
Moves the whole soul,
The whole being.

Not just words, but an
Encounter of
Heart.
Mind.
Feelings.
Emotions.

By Definition

and say,

When you think of all the ways
That we might speak,

It makes sense
To suss out the meaning of "say."

In other definitions, usage, translations:

Speak.
Tell.
Utter.
Affirm.
Teach.
Exhort.
Advise.
Command.
Direct.
Entreat.
Boast.
Call.
Describe.
Name.
Put forth.
Enumerate.
Recount.
Narrate.
Describe.
Make plain.
Unfold.
Explain.
Insist.
Salute.

Worthy

"You are worthy, our Lord and God,
to receive glory and honor and power,
for you created all things,
and by your will they were created
and have their being."

The word "worth"
Is like
A math problem.

The weight of one thing
Compared to
Another thing of like value.

Your worth
Equals
The glory, honor, and power due
For you created all things.

Your worth
Befits
Your magnificence as
Creator and sustainer.

Your merit
Corresponds
With the splendor
Of all things.

For glory and honor and power
You are
Worthy.
Deserving.
Suitable.
Due.

Receive

You are worthy, our Lord and God,
  to receive

Worthy to receive.

Worthy to take hold of any person or thing
  to use it.

Worthy to take your due.
Worthy to gather tribute.

Jesus, take back what's your own.
And don't let go.

Mystery

You are worthy, our Lord and God,
    to receive glory and honor and power,

Notice.

The four living creatures give
Glory,
Honor, and
Thanks.

The twenty-four elders say
Glory,
Honor, and
Power.

Two out of three the same.
One different.

Why?

Do the living creatures
Emphasize his
Goodness,

While the elders
Emphasize his
Creative might?

Perhaps.

A glorious mystery.

Power

You are worthy, our Lord and God,
  to receive glory and honor and power,

From the same root word
That we get *dynamite.*

Mighty work.
Strength.
Miracle.
Might.
Virtue.
Ability.
Abundance.
Meaning.
Force.
Working.
Authority.

It's the inherent power,
The power residing in a thing
By virtue of its nature.

Power for performing miracles.
Moral power and excellence of soul.
The power and influence which belong to riches
  and wealth.
The power and resources arising from numbers.
The power resting upon armies, forces, hosts.[33]

Join In

You are worthy, our Lord and God,
to receive glory and honor and power,

With the elders,
We say:

Worthy,
Oh, master.

Worthy,
Oh, Lord.

Our God, take the
Glory, take the
Honor, take the
Power.

You created it all because
You wanted it all.

Worthy are you.
Amen and amen.

Pleasure

for you created all things,
    and by your will they were created

God did what he wished,
What he determined to do.

He made his choice,
Satisfied his desire,

Created all things
For his pleasure.

Creator

for you created all things,
  and by your will they were created
  and have their being."

We worship you,

Creator and
Sustainer.

You created out of nothing,
Formed and shaped the worlds.

You made the earth
Habitable,

And continue to change
And transform

The world
And all who dwell therein.

Chapter Six
REVELATION 5:1-7

Right Hand

*Then I saw in the right hand of him who sat on the
throne a scroll*

John's attention

Shifts

From throne,
And the one who sits there,

To scroll,

Held in the right hand
Of the enthroned Lord,

Held in the hand of
Authority and
Strength.

Picture This

a scroll

Not a modern sheet of printer paper,
Rolled into a small, light cylinder.

No.

A scroll is made of
Papyrus or vellum,
Reeds or animal skin.

A scroll might unroll to
Fifteen or thirty feet long.

The text, written in columns
A few inches wide,
Revealed column by column.

Heavy, weighty.
Magnificent.

Both Sides

with writing on both sides

Today all books
Have writing on both sides of the paper.

But at the time of John,
This was unusual.

The information on this scroll:
Almost more than the one scroll can contain.

Guesswork

with writing on both sides

Learned scholars debate:
What was written?

The Old Testament?
A proclamation of God's purpose for Israel?

Was it a judgment?
A sentencing against the enemies of God's people?

Was it the text of the book of Revelation?
Or the title deed to the purposes and
　　plans of God?

Biblical historian John Barclay thought
This was God's will,

His final settlement of the affairs of the universe.
God's final verdict revealed.

The consummation of history.
A full account of what God has in store for
　　the world.

Sealed

and sealed with seven seals.

To keep the scroll intact,
Strings wrap the roll around and tie.
Wax covers the knots,
And a seal imprints the wax.

Seven strings, knotted.
Seven beads of wax, dabbed.
Seven times, the seal pressed down.
One scroll ... impenetrable.

Seven

seven

From the time of God's creation,
Where he rested on the seventh day,
The number seven signifies

Completion.
Perfection.
Wholeness.
Holy works of God.

A Mighty Angel

And I saw a mighty angel proclaiming in a loud voice,
  "Who is worthy to break the seals and open the scroll?"

A mighty angel asks a question.

Mighty.
Strong.
Strong in body and mind.
Powerful.
Valiant.
Excellent.

An angel who has the strength of soul
To endure the attacks of the enemy.

This angel asks a question.

No One

*But no one in heaven or on earth or under the earth
could open the scroll or even look inside it.*

Who was worthy?

No one.
Nothing.
None.

No creature
In heaven,
On earth,
Under the earth.

Still sealed securely.

Mourning

I wept and wept because no one was found who was
worthy to open the scroll or look inside.

In the place of magnificence and glory,
John weeps.

What shocking statement is this?
Weeping in heaven?

In the midst of the glory,
John still wept and wept.

The splendor did not prevent him from
Giving full vent to his grief.

All the splendor of the worship,
All the majesty of the throne,

Not enough to distract him
From the lack of worthiness ...

His own lack,
And that of everything else.

Holy.
Mourning.

Comfort

Then one of the elders said to me, "Do not weep! See,
  the Lion of the tribe of Judah, the Root of David,
  has triumphed. He is able to open the scroll and its
  seven seals."

In the midst of grief,
An elder comes to comfort.

Not an angel.
Not a living creature.

Rather, one of the redeemed
Changed John's focus.

No need to weep.
The worthy one has triumphed.

The Lion

See, the Lion of the tribe of Judah,

The Messianic title,
The perfect representation
Of the Messiah.

The excellency of the Lion.
The strength of the Lion.
The roar of the Lion.

The beauty of his look.
The heroic spirit of a champion.
The king of the beasts.

Foretold

the Lion of the tribe of Judah,

When Jacob-turned-Israel
Blessed his sons, he said to Judah,

"You are a lion's cub, Judah;
You return from the prey, my son.
Like a lion he crouches and lies down,
Like a lioness—who dares to rouse him?
The scepter will not depart from Judah,
Nor the ruler's staff from between his feet,
Until he to whom it belongs shall come
And the obedience of the nations shall be his."[34]

The obedience of the nations
Shall be his.

Of the Tribe

the Lion of the tribe of Judah,

The name Judah means
"Praise."

Jesus:
The Lion of the tribe of praise.

The Root of David

the Root of David,

The prophet Isaiah prophesied
Over the family of Jesse, father of David:

A shoot will come up from the stump of Jesse;
From his roots a Branch will bear fruit.
The Spirit of the Lord will rest on him—
The Spirit of wisdom and of understanding,
The Spirit of counsel and of might,
The Spirit of the knowledge and fear of the Lord—
And he will delight in the fear of the Lord.
He will not judge by what he sees with his eyes,
Or decide by what he hears with his ears;
But with righteousness he will judge the needy,
With justice he will give decisions for the poor of
*   the earth.*
In that day the Root of Jesse
Will stand as a banner for the peoples;
The nations will rally to him,
And his resting place will be glorious.[35]

Zechariah took up theme:
"For, behold, I will bring forth my servant the
*   Branch...."*[36]
Thus speaketh the Lord of hosts, saying,
"Behold the man whose name is The Branch;
And he shall grow up out of his place,
And he shall build the temple of the Lord."[37]

To leave no doubt of who this refers to:
"I, Jesus, have sent my angel
To give you this testimony for the churches.
I am the Root and the Offspring of David,
And the bright Morning Star."[38]

Jesus.
The Lion of the tribe of Judah.
The Root of David.

Triumphant

has triumphed. He is able to open the scroll and its seven seals."

The Lion has

Overcome.
Conquered.
Prevailed.
Won the victory.

He defeated all foes.

The one who is worthy.

Unexpected

Then I saw a Lamb,

John looked to see the Lion,
But instead saw a Lamb.

A lambkin,
A little lamb.

An adorable baby lamb,
Tiny and delicate.

Not the animal
He was expecting to see.

Mascot

a Lamb,

Sports teams, schools, nations
Choose symbols of

Strength.
Prowess.
Intensity.
Force.
Ferocity.
Power.
Might.
Aggressiveness.

A lamb stands in opposition
To all worldly expectations of victory.

Humility.
Kindness.
Caring.
Gentleness.
Generosity.
Sweetness.
Sensitivity.

Sacrifice.

Sacrificed

looking as if it had been slain,

The meaning of
"Slain"?

Not, as you might reasonably expect,
The word "killed."

Rather:
Slaughtered.
Butchered in sacrifice.

So what is it that John sees,
In this animal with the marks of sacrifice?

A slit throat,
Like a lamb?

Or a crucified form,
Like a man, with marks of

Thorns,
Whip,

Nails,
Spear?

Weep Not for Me

looking as if it had been slain,

Though the Lamb bore
The marks of sacrifice,

No object of pity
Here.

Do not gaze and
Weep.

Gaze in
Awe.

Fresh Blood

Then I saw a Lamb, looking as if it had been slain,

Though the Lamb was sacrificed years ago,
The blood remains fresh.

Not cold, passive, calloused, stale, hardened.
No.

Fresh.
Powerful.
Effectual.
Offered.

Our great advantage.

Submission

Then I saw a Lamb, looking as if it had been slain,

John the Baptist said of Jesus,
"Look, the Lamb of God,
Who takes away the sin of the world!"[39]

Centuries before, Isaiah, too, prophesied:
He was oppressed and afflicted,
Yet he did not open his mouth;
He was led like a lamb to the slaughter,
And as a sheep before its shearers is silent,
So he did not open his mouth.[40]

In the time of Moses,
A family chose an unblemished lamb,
Killed it, and
Covered the door posts of their house
With its blood.

Here, God himself
Chooses an unblemished Lamb,
Ever submitted to his Father.
Sacrificed on behalf of the people,
His blood poured out
To cover our sins.

Slaughtered: Standing

Then I saw a Lamb, looking as if it had been slain,
standing at the center of the throne, encircled by the
four living creatures and the elders.

Sacrificed animals fall down and lie still.
Inert, immovable, dead.

This slaughtered Lamb, though,
Stands in the center of the throne,

In the midst of
The living creatures and the elders.

Stands ...

Triumphant.

Seven Horns

The Lamb had seven horns

Horns represent the
Power of God.
Authority.
Strength.
Courage.

Seven Eyes

and seven eyes,

Eyes:
Seeing into.
Knowledge.
Wisdom.
Insight.

Three Omnis

The Lamb had seven horns and seven eyes, which are
the seven spirits of God sent out into all the earth.

Seven horns for the
Omnipotence of God,
All power,
Unlimited power,
Only found in God.

Seven eyes for the
Omniscience of God,
All knowing,
Complete knowledge,
Only found in God.

Seven spirits for the
Omnipresence of God,
All presence,
Everywhere at once,
Only found in God.

The Lamb:
All powerful,
All knowing,
All present.
What a God to serve.

Take It

He went and took the scroll from the right hand of him who sat on the throne.

The Lamb took the scroll.

The only one able.

Picture This

He went and took the scroll from the right hand of him
who sat on the throne.

One throne.

God enthroned,
Holding the scroll in his right hand.

Then the proclamation of the Lion,
The vision of the Lamb on the throne.

The Lamb took the scroll.

How can this be?
Does a Lamb have hands?
And isn't the Lamb the same as the one who sat
on the throne?

It's a vision.

Be awed by the majesty,
And think less about
Precision of place and person.

Chapter Seven
REVELATION 5:8–10

Immediate

And when he had taken it, the four living creatures and the twenty-four elders fell down before the Lamb.

Earlier in the scene, the elders
Fall down.

Now the living creatures and the elders
Fall down.

The living creatures and
Redeemed man,
Now partnering
Together
To worship
The Lamb.

Music in Heaven

*Each one had a harp and they were holding golden
bowls full of incense, which are the prayers of
God's people.*

Already we have heard voices.
Now we see harps.

Voices and
Instruments,

Both.

Worship with mouth,
Worship with hands.

Speak truth.
Make music from a full heart.

Instruments

a harp

Not the four-stringed lute,

But

The seven-stringed
Kithara,
An instrument for professionals,
Played in heaven.

When we pray,
"You kingdom come,
Your will be done
On earth
As it is in heaven,"[41]

Let's bring heaven's sound to earth, with
Music and
Melody and
Instruments
Unto the Lord.

Strongest Sense

and they were holding golden bowls full of incense,

Smell is the
Strongest sense.

Intense.

One small whiff
Triggers memory of place.

Smell bypasses the thinking part of the brain,
Goes directly to the emotional part.

Man is made in God's image.
If man remembers with a small smell,

How much more does God?
When he smells the incense, he remembers.

Prayers

which are the prayers of God's people.

The sweet-smelling incense
Ascends.

Let my prayers
Be set before you
As incense,
The lifting up my hands
As the evening sacrifice.[42]

These prayers bring God
Joy and pleasure.

Prayers

which are the prayers of God's people.

God's people cry out to
God.

Between God and man
Stands a mediator, a
Go-between.[43]

The pray-er is never

Alone

When praying,
"Your kingdom come,
Your will be done."

God's People

which are the prayers of God's people.

The prayers of the saints,
The prayers of God's people.

Think of the Desert Fathers,
Crying out in a dry land.

Think of the cathedrals
Full of mystery and awe.

Think of the saints standing outside
During the Great Awakening.

Monasteries and monks,
Pilgrims and pastors,

Mothers with children,
Women ministering.

The ancients and the moderns,
Rural, urban, and suburban.

The prayers of the holy ones,
Ascending.

Harp and Bowl

*Each one had a harp and they were holding golden
    bowls full of incense, which are the prayers of
    God's people.*

Praise and prayer,
Worship and intercession.

Either alone is good.
Both together is better.

Praise to God for all he is.
Praise to God for all he paid for.

Prayer to God for this broken, hurting world.
Prayer to God for his remembrance.

A New Song

And they sang a new song, saying:
"You are worthy to take the scroll
and to open its seals,
because you were slain,
and with your blood you purchased for God
persons from every tribe and language and people
*   and nation.*
You have made them to be a kingdom and priests to
*   serve our God,*
and they will reign on the earth."

The old song celebrated
Holiness,
Creator,
Creation.

The new song celebrates
Worthiness,
Sacrifice,
Redemption,
Transformation.

Worthy

You are worthy

The people said to
The Roman emperors
Vere dignus,
"You are worthy."
Spoken to fallen man.

But here in heaven
The true ruler of the world
Receives his proper worship.
Jesus is worthy.
Spoken to glorified Lamb.

Infinite Contrast

You are worthy

No one in heaven or on earth or under the earth
Could open the scroll.

Recognize man's
Sinfulness and separation,

The vast distance between
A holy God and

Fallen creation.
An infinite contrast.

The broken self
Compared to the holy, set apart, beautiful God.

And yet ...
John received the invitation:

"Come up here."

Receive the touch of God's mercy.

Honor

And they sang a new song, saying:
"You are worthy to take the scroll
and to open its seals,
because you were slain,
and with your blood you purchased for God
persons from every tribe and language and people
and nation.
You have made them to be a kingdom and priests to
serve our God,
and they will reign on the earth."

Honor the calling of redemption:
Sing a new song.

Honor the worker of redemption:
The Lamb of God.

Honor the price of redemption:
The blood of the Lamb.

Honor the destination of redemption:
Redeemed to God.

Honor the payment of redemption:
Jesus's blood applied on man's behalf.

Honor the scope of the redemption:
Every tribe, and language, and people, and nation.

Honor the destiny of redemption:
Made people a kingdom and priests.

Honor the length of redemption:
For ever and ever.

Honor the purpose of redemption:
The glory of God the Father.

Ever New

And they sang a new song,

Dr. Pete Carter talks about
"A continually developing theology."[44]

Because God is eternal and infinite,
There is always more to discover about him.

As we pursue God,
We find always an ever more beautiful vista

Opening before us.
Pleasure without end.

Sing

A new song.

Our Response to the Song

because you were slain,
and with your blood you purchased for God
persons from every tribe and language and people
*   and nation.*

Remember the blessing of the blood,
The power, cleansing, victory of the blood,
The redemption in the blood.

Rejoice in the hope found in God.
Embrace the promises,
Even when they seem far off.

A new song plays in the heavens,
Joyful,
Fresh.

Treasure this excellent song
That proclaims Christ's
Death and

Resurrection.

Only One Effective Salvation

and with your blood you purchased for God
persons from every tribe and language and people
   and nation.

Though some try to save themselves,
Through good works or intellectual pursuits,

In truth,
Salvation belongs to the Lamb.

The languages of the earth
Shall worship you, Jesus.

Salvation belongs to our God.
No one else.

Every

and with your blood you purchased for God
persons from every tribe and language and people
   and nation.

God's people:
Diverse.
One.

God's plan:
Every nation worshiping
Jesus.

Still Going Forth

persons from every tribe and language and people
and nation.

Does the world seem to get darker?
When Christ returned to heaven,
A few hundred followers began to spread the news.

By the time of John's death, the last
surviving apostle,
Several thousands, spread throughout the world.
Not many, really.

The gospel goes forth to this day,
Seeking the lost in every language,
Reaching for the promised global scope.

Kingdom and Priests

You have made them to be a kingdom and priests to
serve our God,

To a people in slavery,
Under tyranny,
Bound by fear,

A radical promise:

Be a kingdom.
Be priests.
Enter the kingdom of unbound promises.

Because of new birth into the family of God,
Because God is our Father,
We enter God's kingdom.

As we praise and pray,
We bring the incense to the altar,
Serving as priests of our God.

Reign

and they will reign on the earth."

Each generations has many priests,
Numerous servants of the Lord.

But kings?
So few.

And yet here we find a message
Of reigning.

What an
Expectation!

Chapter Eight
REVELATION 5:11–14

Angels

Then I looked and heard the voice of many angels,
numbering thousands upon thousands, and ten
thousand times ten thousand. They encircled the
throne and the living creatures and the elders.

Angels help fulfill
God's purpose on the earth.

Deliver a message,[45]
As the angel's announcement to Mary.

Intervene on behalf of God's people,[46]
As the angel stopped the mouth of the lion
   for Daniel.

Offer unexpected encouragement,[47]
As the angel found Hagar in the desert.

Guard God's people,[48]
So we don't strike our foot against a stone.

Guide God's people,[49]
As when the angel of God traveled in front

Israel's army.

Punish justly,[50]
As when the angel destroyed Jerusalem for the sin
of King David.

Encircle God's people,[51]
As the horses and chariots of fire around Elisha.

Fight forces of evil,[52]
As the angelic forces fought the Prince of
Persia 21 days.

Here they have another
Role to fulfill.

Countless angels
Join the song.

Worship the
Lamb.

The Song of the Lamb

In a loud voice they were saying:
"Worthy is the Lamb, who was slain,
* to receive power and wealth and wisdom and strength*
*   and honor and glory and praise!"*

Worthy is the Lamb who was slaughtered.

Prompted

In a loud voice they were saying:

In Revelation 4,
The living creatures worship,
And then the elders follow.

In Revelation 5,
The living creatures and the elders worship,
And then the angels follow.

Think of this glorious cycle of praise,
Where the need to worship overcomes first
   one group,
Then another,

All encouraging each other and
Inspiring each other

To more and

More and

More

Praise.

Similar

"Worthy is the Lamb, who was slain,
to receive power and wealth and wisdom and strength
and honor and glory and praise!"

In the song of Creation,
The elders declared that
The one who sits on the throne
Is worthy of

Glory.
Honor.
Power.

But the one who redeems the lost?
For him,
Proclaim four more magnificent words:

Wealth.
Wisdom.
Strength.
Praise.

Wealth

wealth

From a root word meaning
Fill.
Accomplish.
Furnish.
Supply.

Think:
Fullness of wealth.
Abundance of possessions.
Plenty.
Richness.
Valuable bestowment.

No Poverty in Heaven

wealth

Don't take a vow of poverty
To be more like Jesus.

Though he had no permanent home
While he ministered on earth,

His robe was fine enough
That soldiers gambled to win it.

Though he made himself nothing
To become a man,[53]

His lives in
A glorious home in heaven,

And his followers worship him,
Proclaiming his worth for more abundance.

Sophia

wisdom

From the root word meaning
Clear.
Wise.
Skilled.

Forming the best plans with the best execution.

The word *Sophia* means
"Wisdom."

Broad and full of intelligence.

Knowledge of very diverse matters:
Human and divine,
Acquired by acuteness and experience,
Summed up in maxims and proverbs,
Science and learning,
Dream interpretation,
Giving sage advice,
Searching out the meaning of some mysterious
    number or vision,
Skillful management of affairs,
Prudence in dealing with those not yet in the fold,
Skill and discretion when imparting
Christian truth,
Knowing and practicing the essentials of godly
    and upright living.

Supreme intelligence that belongs to God.

The wisdom of God that forms and
    executes counsels
In the formation and government of the world
    and the scriptures.

Surprise

wisdom

The heavenly host
Proclaims that Jesus is worthy
To receive
Wisdom.

Hebrews tells us,
By faith we understand that
The universe was formed at God's command,
So that what is seen
Was not made out of what was visible.[54]

The created order is so
Orderly—

What a surprising thought,
That Jesus is worthy of wisdom,

When he already has
So much.

Perhaps we should always seek
For more of truly good things.

Strength

strength

From the root word meaning
To have.
To hold.
To possess.

Here the heavenly host proclaims
Forcefulness.
Ability.
Might.
Strength.

Think physicality,
As in:
Thou shalt love the Lord thy God
With all thy heart, and
With all thy soul, and
With all thy mind, and
With all thy

Strength.[55]

Again, Surprised

strength

Because Jesus had
No stately form or majesty
To attract us,[56]
It's easy enough to overlook
Any need for strength.

And yet ...
Surely he has borne our griefs
And carried our sorrows.[57]

He bears heavy weight
So our shoulders remain
Unburdened.

Indeed:
Proclaim strength over this
Savior.

Blessing

praise!

From the Greek meaning
Good word.
Well done word.
Eulogy.

Translated also
Blessing.
Bounty.
Bountifully.
Fair speech.

The heavenly host say Jesus is worthy to receive:
Fine speaking.
Elegance of language.
Commendation.
Adoration.
Benediction.
Consecration.
Benefit.

Yes.
Worthy.

Outstanding

praise!

When you read the Gospels,
Over and over
Jesus unexpectedly
Confounds the wise.

Apparently the cries for
Supreme intelligence and fine speaking
Began to be answered
Before they were asked.

Variety

Then I heard every creature in heaven and on earth
and under the earth and on the sea, and all that is in
them, saying:
"To him who sits on the throne and to the Lamb
be praise and honor and glory and power,
for ever and ever!"

Every creature speaks out.
Thousands of human languages,
Plus all the creatures.

Think of the variety of
Rhythms.
Melodies.
Harmonies.
Sounds.
Syllables.

Come and worship the
Lamb.

One

*Then I heard every creature in heaven and on earth
and under the earth and on the sea, and all that
is in them,*

In the midst of worshiping God:
Incredible unity among his creation.

Think of the relationship between Father
and the Son:
They are

One.[58]

In heaven, even the form of worship
Reflects God's heart.

Locations

Then I heard every creature in heaven and on earth
and under the earth and on the sea,

To make sure all understand the word
"Every,"
John spells it out.

Every created being:

Those in heaven.
Those on earth.
Those beneath the earth's surface.
Those in the sea.

Humility

every creature

Paul, too, wrote about every tongue
Worshiping.

And being found in appearance as a man,
He humbled himself
By becoming obedient to death—
Even death on a cross!
Therefore God exalted him to the highest place
And gave him the name that is above every name,
That at the name of Jesus every knee should bow,
In heaven and on earth and under the earth,
And every tongue acknowledge that Jesus Christ is Lord,
To the glory of God the Father.[59]

Jesus humbled himself and
God exalted him.

He went lower and
God raised him higher.

Humility Again

every creature

Humble servant,
Humble teacher,

Now portrayed as the
All powerful King,
Victorious in

All things,
All seasons,
All times,
All situations.

Glorious.

The power of Christ,
The resurrected one,
Strong,
Conqueror,
Preeminent,

Over all, and
Through all, and
In all.[60]

Power

power

From a root meaning
To perfect.
To complete.

Yes, also
Might.
Strength.
Force.

But also

Great vigor.

And, especially,

Dominion.

Christus Victor

"To him who sits on the throne and to the Lamb
be praise and honor and glory and power,
for ever and ever!"

God holds the future
In complete control.

From the beginning,
When he created all,

To the present,
When his purpose goes forth,

To the ages and ages to come ...
He reigns.

For Ever

for ever and ever!"

The living God
Reigns
For ever and ever.

Kings come and kings go.
Kingdoms come and kingdoms go.

But the kingdom of God
Remains

For ever.

The Lord God lives
Ever worthy of praise,

For ever.

Worship him

For ever and ever.

Amen

*The four living creatures said, "Amen," and the elders
  fell down and worshiped.*

The word *Amen*:
Called "the best known word in human speech."[61]

Transliterated from Hebrew into Greek,
From Greek into Latin,
Then into English and other languages,
A universal word.

Surely.
Truly.
So it is.
So be it.

May it be fulfilled.

POSTSCRIPT

In Harmony

Did you notice,
In all of the activity around the throne, the
Peaceful,
Beautiful
Order?

Not chaotic.
Not confusing.
Colorful.

Harmony.
Unity.
Proper sequence.

Delight in
The structure,
The form,
The precision of
God's kingdom.

For God is not a God of disorder
But of
Peace.[62]

Orthodox

In the West, people learn about Jesus
Through the Word.

But in the East, people learn about Jesus
Through imagery.

Picture the walls of an Orthodox Church.

Face the front and see
The four evangelists,
Matthew, Mark, Luke, and John,
Together with the people in the gospels.

On the right and on the left, see
Peter and Paul and
Their exploits in Acts.

But on the back wall,
Around the door, see
The stories of Revelation:

The coming of the kingdom,
The coming of Christ,
The glory of the resurrected one.

Is the news of the day gloomy?

Face the stories of Revelation
Before the exit into the world.

Remember that God's plan for the future
Will
Come to pass.

Jesus
Will
Conquer evil.

Victory

Though later in Revelation
We see the showdown between
God and his enemy,
Called "the god of this age,"[63]

Have no doubt of the outcome:

God is the ultimate champion.

Of the greatness of his government and peace
There will be no end.
He will reign on David's throne
And over his kingdom,
Establishing and upholding it
With justice and righteousness
From that time on and forever.
The zeal of the Lord Almighty
Will accomplish this.[64]

Step Forward

Appointed and
Anointed,

The risen Lord
Now empowers his people
To make a difference.

Join the song of heaven and
Bring about hope and faith.

Bring God's heart and kingdom
Into the world.

Eagerly step forward to
A life called and marked
By the distinction of the great I Am.

Respond to the
Heavenly call of
His splendor and
His beauty.

The Solution

From distracted worship,
This invitation reveals another way.

God's presence gives:
Perfect joy.
Incredible peace.
Purpose.
Fulfillment.

Distraction-free worship.
Focus.
Awe.

The whole body, every sense,
Energized.

The supernatural ability to
Comprehend
The loving God.

Creator.
Sustainer.
Savior.
Lord.
King.

CONCLUSION

Out Loud

Paul instructed Timothy:

Until I come,
Devote yourself to the public reading of Scripture,
To preaching and to teaching.[65]

Historically,
The fellowship of believers
Read the scriptures
Out loud.

The vision of the throne room:

Not a somber, quiet place,
But one full of
Excitement,
Activity,
Passion.

Your turn now:
Pray and sing these words

Out
Loud.

REVELATION 4-5

After this I looked, and there before me was a door standing open
in heaven. And the voice I had first heard speaking to me like a
trumpet said, "Come up here, and I will show you what must take
place after this." At once I was in the Spirit, and there before me
was a throne in heaven with someone sitting on it.
And the one who sat there had the appearance of jasper and ruby.
A rainbow that shone like an emerald encircled the throne. Surrounding the throne were twenty-four other thrones, and seated
on them were twenty-four elders. They were dressed in white and
had crowns of gold on their heads. From the throne came flashes of
lightning, rumblings and peals of thunder. In front of the throne,
seven lamps were blazing. These are the seven spirits of God. Also
in front of the throne there was what looked like a sea of glass, clear
as crystal.
In the center, around the throne, were four living creatures, and they
were covered with eyes, in front and in back. The first living creature was like a lion, the second was like an ox, the third had a face
like a man, the fourth was like a flying eagle. Each of the four living
creatures had six wings and was covered with eyes all around, even
under its wings. Day and night they never stop saying:
"'Holy, holy, holy is the Lord God Almighty,'
who was, and is, and is to come."
Whenever the living creatures give glory, honor and thanks to
him who sits on the throne and who lives for ever and ever, the
twenty-four elders fall down before him who sits on the throne
and worship him who lives for ever and ever. They lay their crowns

before the throne and say:
"You are worthy, our Lord and God,
to receive glory and honor and power,
for you created all things, and by your will they were created
and have their being."

Then I saw in the right hand of him who sat on the throne a scroll
with writing on both sides and sealed with seven seals. And I saw a
mighty angel proclaiming in a loud voice, "Who is worthy to break
the seals and open the scroll?" But no one in heaven or on earth or
under the earth could open the scroll or even look inside it. I wept
and wept because no one was found who was worthy to open the
scroll or look inside. Then one of the elders said to me, "Do not
weep! See, the Lion of the tribe of Judah, the Root of David, has
triumphed. He is able to open the scroll and its seven seals."

Then I saw a Lamb, looking as if it had been slain, standing at the
center of the throne, encircled by the four living creatures and the
elders. The Lamb had seven horns and seven eyes, which are the
seven spirits of God sent out into all the earth. He went and took
the scroll from the right hand of him who sat on the throne. And
when he had taken it, the four living creatures and the twenty-four
elders fell down before the Lamb. Each one had a harp and they
were holding golden bowls full of incense, which are the prayers of
God's people. And they sang a new song, saying:
"You are worthy to take the scroll
and to open its seals,
because you were slain,
and with your blood you purchased for God
persons from every tribe and language and people and nation.
You have made them to be a kingdom and priests to serve our God,
and they will reign on the earth."

Then I looked and heard the voice of many angels, numbering thousands upon thousands, and ten thousand times ten thousand. They
encircled the throne and the living creatures and the elders. In a
loud voice they were saying:
"Worthy is the Lamb, who was slain,

to receive power and wealth and wisdom and strength
and honor and glory and praise!"
Then I heard every creature in heaven and on earth and under the
earth and on the sea, and all that is in them, saying:
"To him who sits on the throne and to the Lamb
be praise and honor and glory and power,
for ever and ever!"
The four living creatures said, "Amen," and the elders fell down and
worshiped.

ABOUT THE AUTHORS

Bob Perry has been a passionate student of prayer for more than four decades, constantly asking, "Lord, teach me to pray." He has founded and led multiple prayer initiatives that have trained and mobilized hundreds of thousands of people in prayer partnerships.

Amy Joy Lykosh loves healing and deliverance. Her heart's cry comes from the verse, "My people are destroyed for lack of knowledge" (Hosea 4:6). The author of several highly acclaimed books, she seeks to stop the destruction as best she can through writing and speaking.

Together, they run Workplace Prayer, to cover businesses in prayer, and Prayer Mentoring, to raise up healthy intercessors to bring the kingdom of God to bear in their lives and communities.

NOTES

1   Westminster Shorter Catechism.
2   Matthew 6:10
3   Mark 4:12
4   Proverbs 25.2
5   Revelation 11:15
6   Hebrew 13:8
7   Psalm 27:4
8   Revelation 1:1
9   Revelation 1:3
10 My understanding of this word comes
    from Misreading Scripture with
    Western Eyes, p. 75
11 Revelation 1:10; 4:2; 17:3; 21:10
12 II Peter 1:20-21
13 Daniel 7:13-14
14 Exodus 19:20, 24
15 Psalm 47:8
16 I Kings 22:19
17 Ezekiel 1:26
18 Isaiah 6:1
19 Ezekiel 1:26-28
20 Exodus 19:16
21 Psalm 77:18
22 From Zechariah 4:1-6
23 The Passion Translation, by
    Brian Simmons
24 Ezekiel 1:5-9, 13-14, 18
25 Isaiah 6:2
26 Isaiah 10:12
27 Matthew 11:29
28 Isaiah 6:3
29 Hebrews 13:8
30 https://www.blueletterbible.
    org/lang/lexicon/lexicon.
    cfm?Strongs=G1391&t=KJV
31 Daniel 4:34
32 Daniel 6:26
33 https://www.blueletterbible.
    org/lang/lexicon/lexicon.
    cfm?Strongs=G1411&t=KJV
34 Genesis 49:9-10
35 Isaiah 11:1-4; 10
36 Zechariah 3:8, KJV
37 Zechariah 6:12, KJV
38 Revelation 22:16
39 John 1:29
40 Isaiah 53:7
41 Matthew 6:10
42 Psalm 141:2
43 "For there is one God and one mediator
    between God and mankind, the man
    Christ Jesus," I Timothy 2:5
44 Chasing Lazarus, Dr. Pete Carter, p. 82
45 Luke 1:26-28
46 Daniel 6:22
47 Genesis 16:7
48 Psalm 91:11-12
49 Exodus 14:19
50 II Samuel 24:16
51 II Kings 6:17
52 Daniel 10:13
53 Philippians 2:7
54 Hebrews 11:3
55 Mark 12:30, KJV
56 Isaiah 53:2, Berean Study Bible
57 Isaiah 53:4, NKJV
58 John 17:21
59 Philippians 2:8-11
60 Ephesians 4:6
61 https://www.blueletterbible.
    org/lang/lexicon/lexicon.
    cfm?Strongs=G281&t=KJV
62 I Corinthians 14:33
63 II Corinthians 4:4
64 Isaiah 9:7
65 I Timothy 4:13